Places We Live

Living in a
City

Ellen Labrecque

heinemann
raintree

To contact Capstone Global Library, please call 800-747-4992, or visit our web site www.capstonepub.com

Edited by James Benefield and Brenda Haugen
Designed by Richard Parker
Illustrations by HL Studios
Original illustrations © Capstone Global Library Ltd 2015
Picture research by Jo Miller
Production by Helen McCreath
Originated by Capstone Global Library Ltd
Printed and bound in China by Leo Paper Group

18 17 16 15 14
10 9 8 7 6 5 4 3 2 1

Library of Congress Cataloging-in-Publication Data
Labrecque, Ellen.
  Living in a city / Ellen Labrecque.—1 Edition.
     pages cm.—(Places we live)
  Includes bibliographical references and index.
  ISBN 978-1-4846-0805-0 (hb)—ISBN 978-1-4846-0812-8 (pb)—ISBN 978-1-4846-0826-5 (ebook) 1. Cities and towns—Juvenile literature. 2. City and town life—Juvenile literature. I. Title.

  HT119.L337 2015
  307.76—dc23   2014013618

This book has been officially leveled by using the F&P Text Level Gradient™ Leveling System.

Acknowledgments
We would like to thank the following for reproducing photographs: Alamy: Guy Croft, 20, Marcelo Rudini, 21, Travel Pictures, 17; Getty Images: Photolibrary/Robin Smith, 15; Newscom: akg-images, 8, Danita Delimont Photography/Jaynes Gallery/Bill Young, 10, Getty Images/ AFP/Peter Parks, 25; Shutterstock: Ana Phelps, 23, Shutterstock/claudio zaccherini, 26, Shutterstock/Eric Broder Van Dyke, 13, Shutterstock/ EUROPHOTOS, 4, Shutterstock/gary yim, 11, Shutterstock/Lewis Tse Pui Lung, 24, Shutterstock/Lukiyanova Natalia / frenta, 19, Shutterstock/Mazzzur, 12, Shutterstock/nodff, 18, Shutterstock/Pete Spiro, 27, Shutterstock/ptnphoto, 5, Shutterstock/serato, 16, Shutterstock/testing, cover, Shutterstock/Vacclav, 9; SuperStock: age fotostock/Tibor Bognár, 7; UIG via Getty Images: Education Images, 22

Design Elements: Shutterstock: donatas1205, Olympus

We would like to thank Rachel Bowles for her invaluable help in the preparation of this book.

007166LEOS15

Contents

Some words are shown in bold, **like this**. You can find out what they mean by looking in the glossary.

What Is a City?

A city is an **urban settlement**. Lots of people work and live close together here. There are lots of important things here, too. This could include **places of worship**, universities, stores, museums, and company and **government** offices.

Over 13 million people live in the center of Tokyo, Japan.

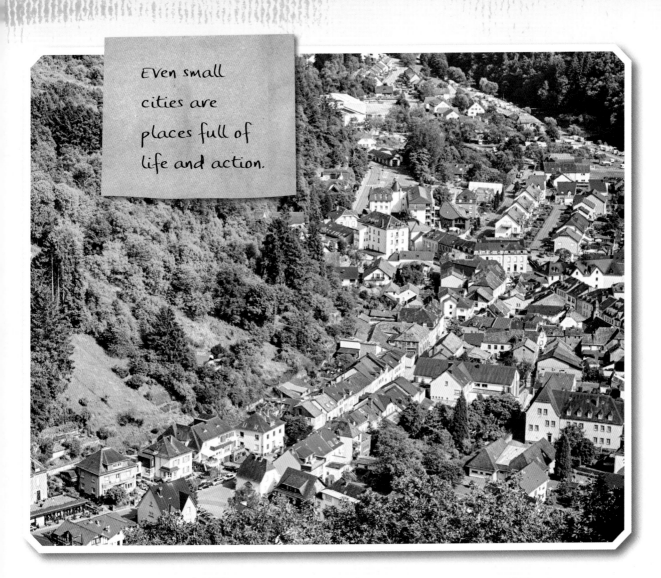

Even small cities are places full of life and action.

Cities mean different things to people around the world. People who live in **rural** areas could call a place with 5,000 people a city. In some areas of the world, 5,000 people might fill just one school or office building.

Where Are Cities?

Cities start in places that meet people's basic needs. For example, every city needs water for its people. This means many cities are built near rivers. Rivers provide water as well as transportation for the people who live there.

Cities with the most people

		Population
1.	Tokyo, Japan	13,300,000
2.	Seoul, South Korea	10,000,000
3.	Jakarta, Indonesia	9,500,000

The city of Seoul, Korea, is built beside the Han River.

City people need food to eat, too. A city built near water means nearby land is usually **fertile**. Gardens and farms can grow vegetables for city people. If city people need anything else, boats and ships can transport this to them.

Cities of the Past

In early times, many cities were built on hills or near water. If enemies tried to attack, they could easily be seen from the hills or in the water. Rome and Jerusalem are cities that were first built long ago. They were both built on hills.

Ancient Rome was built on hills and had a river running through it.

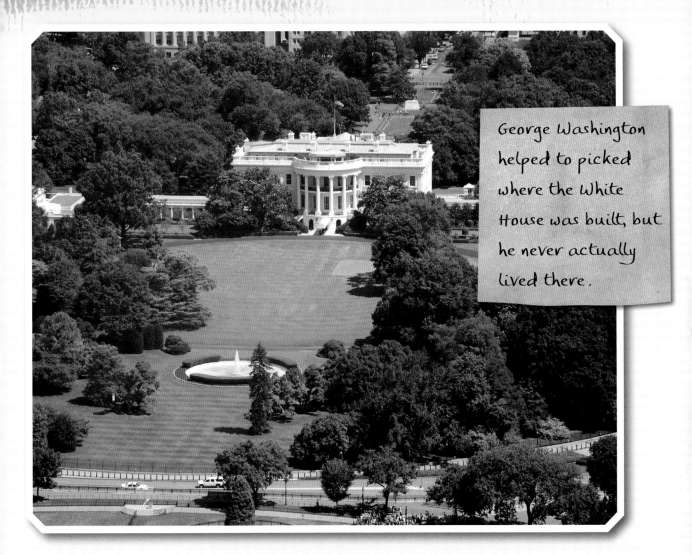

George Washington helped to picked where the White House was built, but he never actually lived there.

Some cities were built by the people in power at the time. The first president of the USA, George Washington, helped to pick Washington DC as the capital city. It was near to where he already lived.

Why Do People Live in Cities Today?

People often move to cities because they could offer people better lives. For example, a city has a better variety of jobs than a **rural** area. Many cities also have excellent schools and universities.

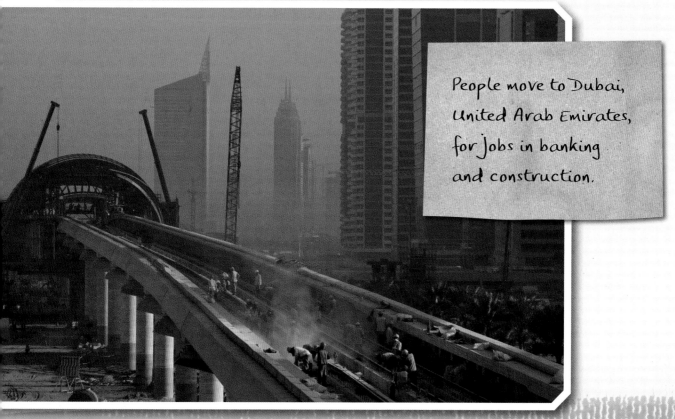

People move to Dubai, United Arab Emirates, for jobs in banking and construction.

You don't need to worry about traffic if you're taking this monorail in Sydney, Australia.

There are lots of ways to get around in cities. You can take public transportation to places inside the city or outside of it. There can be many roads for people with cars, too. But if a city is crowded, there can be traffic problems.

All Kinds of People

Over half of the people in the world live in cities. They are filled with both rich and poor people. Some of the richest people in the world live right next to some of the poorest people.

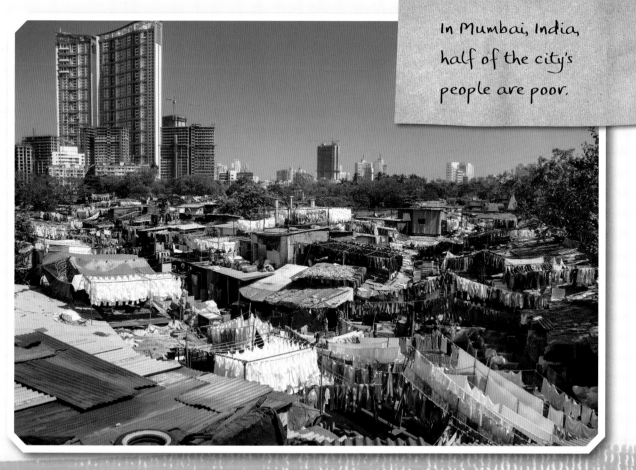

In Mumbai, India, half of the city's people are poor.

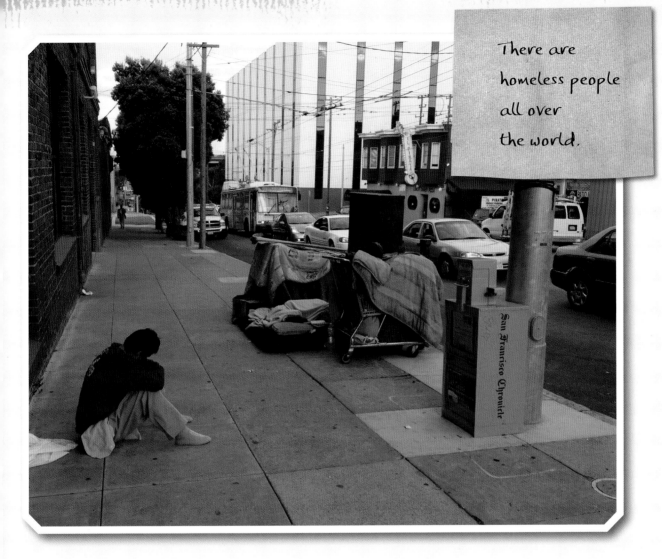

There are homeless people all over the world.

Some rich city people live in large, expensively built homes. Very poor people live in tiny **slums** they have built themselves using scrap material. The poorest could be homeless and live on the streets.

City Puzzle

Cities are made up of different parts. They fit together like giant jigsaw puzzles. The center of a city usually has offices for businesses and **government**. There are also large areas for shopping and entertainment.

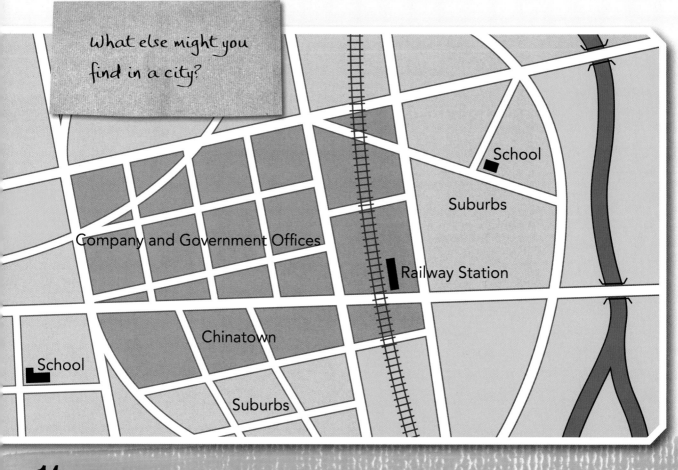

What else might you find in a city?

School

Suburbs

Company and Government Offices

Railway Station

Chinatown

School

Suburbs

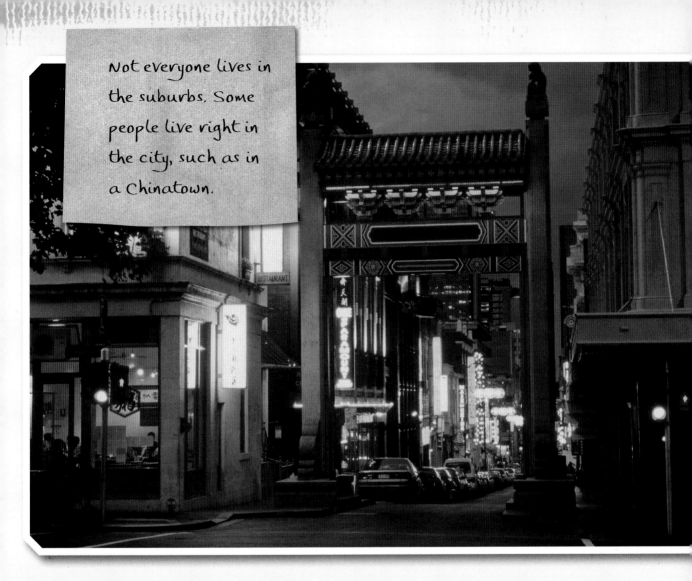

Not everyone lives in the suburbs. Some people live right in the city, such as in a Chinatown.

Towns or areas that are located outside a city are called **suburbs**. This is where a lot of people's homes are. Many people live in the suburbs and come into the center of a city to work. These people are called **commuters**.

Under Our Feet

In big cities, there are things happening underground, too. For example, when people flush a toilet, the water and waste end up in small underground tunnels called **sewers**.

City planners are always careful to keep drinking water pipes separate from waste pipes.

Some big cities have underground transportation systems called subways. This cuts down on traffic on crowded city streets. It can be the quickest way to get around, too. You don't get traffic jams underground.

Buildings and Landmarks

Sometimes city buildings are bult tall because there is not much space. Office and living space is added by building up, not out! The tallest building in the world is the Burj Khalifa in the city of Dubai, United Arab Emirates.

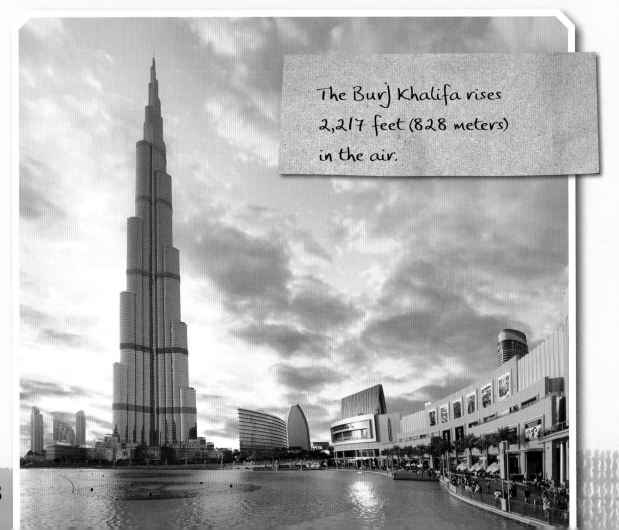

The Burj Khalifa rises 2,217 feet (828 meters) in the air.

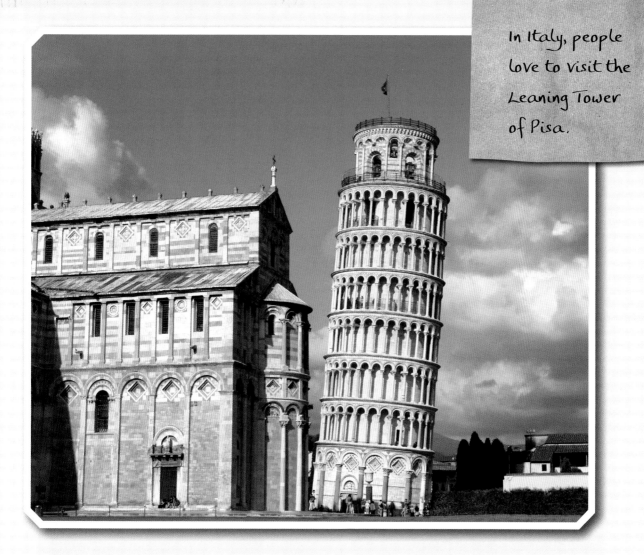

In Italy, people love to visit the Leaning Tower of Pisa.

Tourists like to visit cities to see famous **landmarks**. Tourists stay in the city's hotels and eat in the restaurants. They buy gifts to remember their visits. This all helps to make cities richer.

Open Spaces

Even though cities are crowded, people have built or kept space for parks, gardens, and even beaches. Central Park in New York City is one of the most famous **green spaces** found in a city in the whole world.

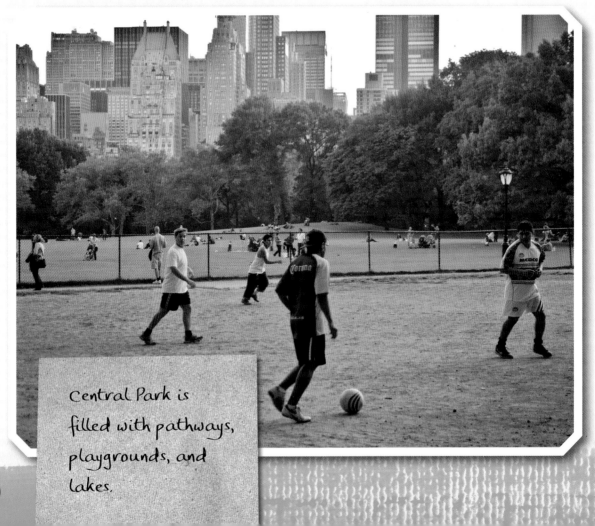

Central Park is filled with pathways, playgrounds, and lakes.

Curitiba, Brazil, has increased green space from 11 square feet per person to 560 square feet per person in 30 years!

City planners are now trying to create more and more green spaces than before. Parks and lakes make people relaxed and give them places to exercise to stay healthy, too.

Fun Things to Do

Cities are packed with fun things to do. For example, they are home to some great zoos. The Moscow Zoo in Moscow, Russia, has over 6,000 animals. Cities also have many great museums and indoor places to play.

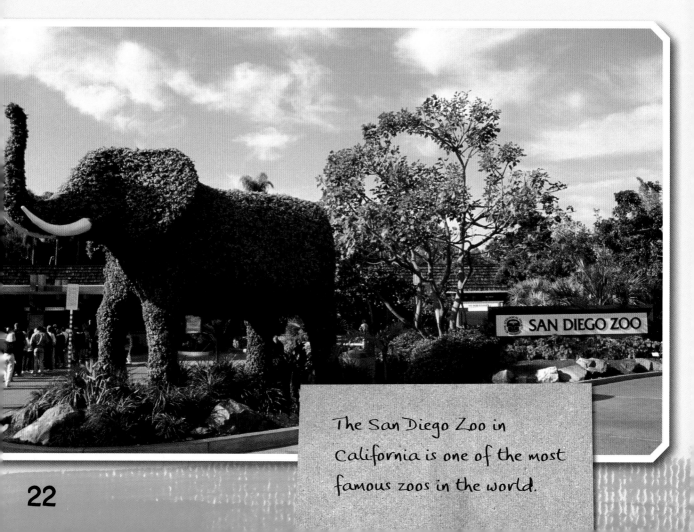

The San Diego Zoo in California is one of the most famous zoos in the world.

The 2016 Olympics in Rio de Janeiro, Brazil, have brought lots of attention to the city.

Cities host all kinds of events, from concerts to sports competitions. When a city hosts a special event, lots of new buildings are built, such as stadiums.

City Life

Living in a city can be exciting, but hard, too. Sometimes it is difficult to find a home that is **affordable** and big enough for the entire family. Many cities are crowded. This can make it hard to walk or drive from one place to another.

Cities are filled with many people fighting for the same space.

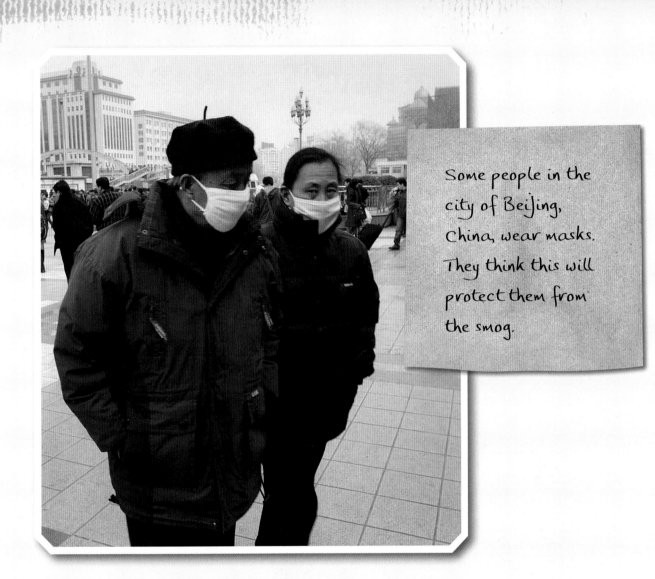

Some people in the city of Beijing, China, wear masks. They think this will protect them from the smog.

Cities can also harm people's health. Sometimes the air in cities becomes polluted by traffic and factories. **Smog** can hang over cities, making it hard to breathe and causing people to get sick.

Cities of the Future

Cities are now very crowded. In 1900, only 16 cities had more than 1 million people living in them. Today, there are more than 400 cities with this many people. What will happen when there are too many people?

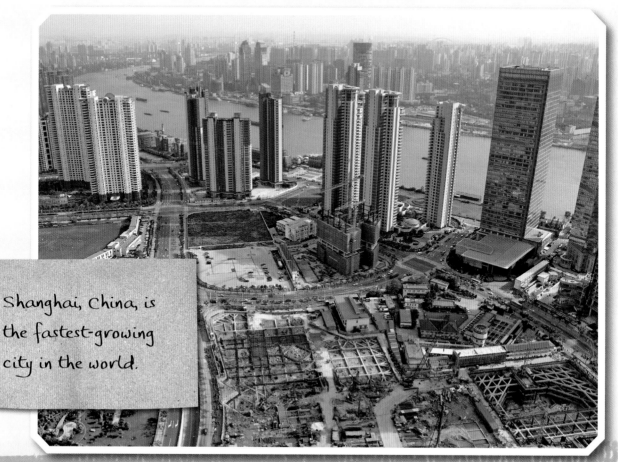

Shanghai, China, is the fastest-growing city in the world.

City planners work to improve cities and make them "greener" places to live. This means they try to cut down on the city's waste. They build new buildings that use **solar power** instead of power from gas, oil, or coal.

Fun Facts

- London (England), Paris (France), New York City (United States), and Bangkok (Thailand) are the most visited cities in the world.

- Washington, D.C., is a city that was built on swampland.

- The London Underground system is called the Tube. It was the world's first subway system.

- A megacity is a city with more than 10 million people living in it. Tokyo, in Japan, and Seoul, in South Korea, are both megacities.

- Singapore, in Southeast Asia, is a city and a country! It is called a city-state.

- Vatican City is also a city-state. It is also the smallest country in the world. It is located inside the city of Rome, Italy.

Quiz

Are each of these sentences true or false?

1. People live in cities because they like to enjoy the wide-open spaces.
2. Towns and areas right outside a city are called suburbs.
3. Central Park in New York City is packed with buildings.
4. There is nothing fun to do in cities.
5. In the past, cities were built on hills.

5. True. This made it easier to protect if the city came under attack.

4. False. The city is filled with fun things for kids to do.

3. False. Central Park is a wide-open green space.

2. True.

1. False. People live in cities because it is easy to find and do all the things they want.

Glossary

affordable something people have enough money to buy

commuter person who travels some way between home and work

fertile land that can grow food, usually with deep and good soil

government group of people who run a city, town, or country

green space parks and other open areas with lots of grass, plants, and trees

landmark famous building, structure, or green space

place of worship religious building for people to pray and meet in

rural area outside a city or town, usually farmland with few people and buildings

settlement place where people live permanently, such as a village, town, or city

sewer underground passageway carrying people's poo and pee

slum overcrowded area where poor people live, often without running water and electricity

smog fog combined with air pollution, which is harmful to health

solar power energy that uses the sun's rays to make electricity

suburb town or area right outside of a city, where people live

tourist person who visits another place for fun

urban relating to living in a town or city

Find Out More

Books

Kent, Peter. Peter Kent's City Across Time.
    New York: Kingfisher, 2010.

Learn About Urban Life (series).
    New York: Crabtree, 2010.

Noon, Steve, and Philip Steele. A City Through Time.
    New York: Dorling Kindersley, 2013.

Steele, Philip. City (DK Eyewitness). New York:
    Dorling Kindersley, 2011.

Internet sites

Facthound offers a safe, fun way to find Internet sites related to this book. All of the sites on Facthound have been researched by our staff.

Here's all you do:

Visit www.facthound.com

Type in this code: 9781484608050

Index